MYSTERIOUS PYRAMIDS

Teotihuacán: *Pyramids of Ancient Mesoamerica*

Murray "Oak" Tapeta

A Crabtree Crown Book

Crabtree Publishing
crabtreebooks.com

Teaching Tips for Caregivers:

You can help your child learn by encouraging them to read widely, both as a leisure activity and as a way of satisfying their curiosity about the world. Reading helps build a strong foundation in language and literacy skills that will help your child succeed in school. This high-interest book will appeal to all readers in intermediate and middle school grades.

Use the following suggestions to help your child grow as a reader.

- Encourage them to read independently at home.
- Encourage them to practice reading aloud.
- Encourage activities that require reading.
- Establish a regular reading time.
- Have your child ask and answer questions about what they read.

Teaching Tips for Teachers:

Engage students throughout the reading process by asking questions like these.

Before Reading

- Ask, "What do you already know about this topic?"
- Ask, "What do you want to learn about this topic?"

During Reading

- Ask, "What is the author trying to teach you?"
- Ask, "How is this like something you have read or seen before?"
- Ask, "How do the text features (headings, index, etc.) help you understand the topic?"

After Reading

- Ask, "What is an interesting fact that you learned about Teotihuacán or early civilizations?"
- Ask, "What questions do you still have about Teotihuacán? How could you find the answers?"

TABLE OF CONTENTS

A Puzzle from the Past....4
Pyramid Styles....6
Ancients Discovering Ancients....8
Mystery City....10
Tremendous Trio....14
The Pyramid of the Sun....16
The Pyramid of the Moon....18
The Temple of the Feathered Serpent....20
Rule of the Aztecs....24
Teotihuacán Lost Again....26
A Walk through History....28
Glossary....30
Index....31
Questions After Reading....31
About the Author....32

A PUZZLE FROM THE PAST

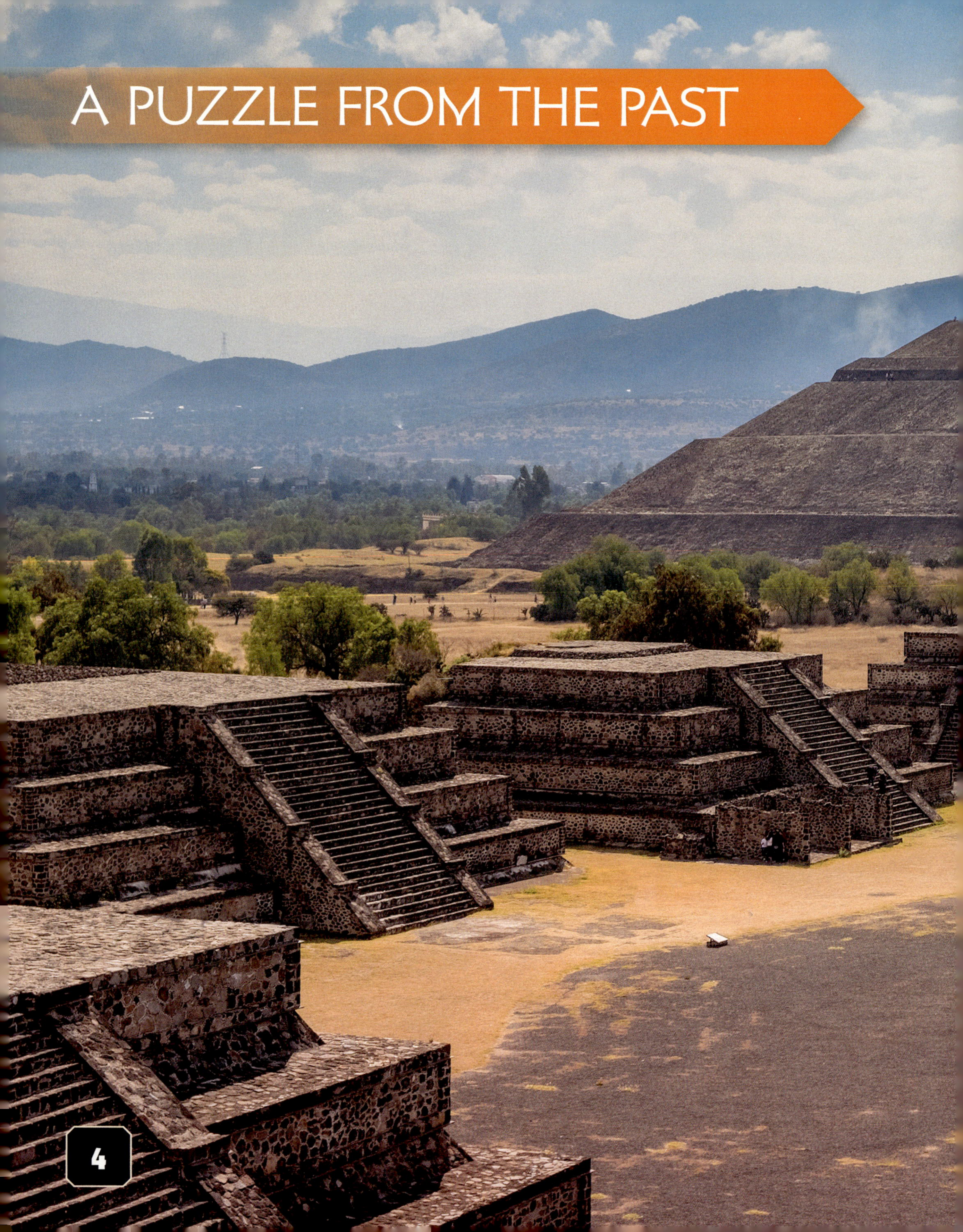

The world is full of mysterious places that hold the secrets of lost **civilizations**. Ancient ruins are like snapshots in time. They provide us with important clues about what life was like long, long ago.

Pyramids usually served as grand burial chambers for royalty or as temples for religious ceremonies or both. These structures exist in various forms around the world, built by civilizations that had little or no contact with one another.

The ruins of the ancient city called Teotihuacán in central Mexico feature three impressive stepped pyramids called the Pyramid of the Sun, the Pyramid of the Moon, and the Temple of the Feathered Serpent.

PYRAMID STYLES

The pyramids of Teotihuacán are step pyramids. These kinds of pyramids have terraces, or flat platforms, and stairways. The pyramids at Teotihuacán were built in a style called talud-tablero. The talud is a sloping wall and the tablero is a vertical panel topped with a platform on top of the slope.

The pyramids are made from local volcanic rock. The ancient city stands near an extinct volcano called Cerro Gordo.

Tikal - Step pyramid

Teotihuacán - Talud-tablero pyramid

- 2600 BCE — Giza
- 2500 BCE
- 2100 BCE — Ziggurat of Ur
- 2000 BCE
- 900 BCE — Tikal
- 259 BCE — Qin Emperor

Giza - True pyramid

Ziggurat of Ur - Step pyramid

Borobudur - Step pyramid

Qin Emperor - Buried flat-topped, step pyramid

Built to Impress!

Why did so many different ancient cultures build similar towering shapes? Relying on the forces of nature, ancient builders learned that the taller you build, the bigger you had to make the base. This helped distribute the weight more toward the bottom so a very tall structure would not topple over.

210 BCE

100 CE

Teotihuacán

450 CE

778 CE

Borobudur

850 CE

900 CE

ANCIENTS DISCOVERING ANCIENTS

Modern-day **archaeologists** uncover treasures from the past. It was no different for ancient explorers. They found objects, buildings, and even entire cities and societies from a time long before their own. This is what happened with the city of Teotihuacán. The Aztecs were one of the great civilizations of the Americas. Their empire lasted from 1345 to 1521 CE. They were known for their military conquests, engineering knowledge, and worship of many gods.

The Aztecs were also explorers. In the 15th century, they came across an abandoned **metropolis** in an area that is now central Mexico. There, perched on a **plateau** in a great valley, stood three large pyramids along with many other structures. The Aztecs called the city Teotihuacán (tay-oh-tee-wah-KAHN)."

The Aztecs had no knowledge of the civilization that came before them. They assumed that Teotihuacán had been built by gods. It became a holy place to them.

MYSTERY CITY

Similar to modern cities, Teotihuacán was arranged in a grid. The city had apartment buildings and palaces. It had temples and plazas. Ancient engineers rerouted the San Juan River so that it flowed right through the city. A main street runs through the center of town. The Aztecs named it *Calle de los Muertos*, or Avenue of the Dead. The avenue is 130 feet (40 meters) wide and runs for 1.2 miles (2.4 kilometers).

Rising up at the north end of the avenue is the great Pyramid of the Moon. At the south end is a courtyard known as the *Ciudadela*, or Citadel. It covers 38 acres (15 hectares). Inside stands a short pyramid called the Temple of Quetzalcóatl or the Temple of the Feathered Serpent. Toward the center of the avenue is the largest pyramid, the magnificent Pyramid of the Sun.

Many of Teotihuacán's buildings have marks showing that they were deliberately burned sometime in the seventh century. Experts think the damage may have been done when poor citizens fought against the rich. By 750 CE, the city was mostly abandoned.

The truth is that not much is known about the builders of Teotihuacán. There is no written record of their history. Experts have pieced together details about this unidentified civilization based on clues they left behind. Historians think that people settled in Teotihuacán as early as 400 BCE. The city's grand structures were built between the first and seventh centuries CE. The buildings spread across eight square miles (20 square kilometers). As many as 200,000 people may have lived in Teotihuacán. It was once one of the largest cities in the world and the first metropolis in the Americas.

TREMENDOUS TRIO

Once, people based many of their beliefs on the movement of heavenly bodies. Standing at the tops of pyramids, ancient **priests** and scientists would study the stars. The three great pyramids at Teotihuacán—the Pyramid of the Sun, the Pyramid of the Moon, and the Temple of the Feathered Serpent—hold many secrets. One of their greatest surprises is that they have nothing inside. Many ancient pyramids around the world contain chambers for the tombs of kings or other important people. This is not true of the Teotihuacán pyramids.

The people of Teotihuacán may have believed that life began underground. In recent years, tunnels have been discovered around and underneath the pyramids. The Pyramid of the Sun itself is built over top of a cave. This leads historians to think the structures may have been intended as a link to the **underworld**.

***Excavations** within the city have not uncovered burial sites for any of the city's rulers.*

THE PYRAMID OF THE SUN

The mountain-shaped Pyramid of the Sun was probably built around 200 CE. It stands 216 feet (66 meters) tall. The rectangular base is 720 by 760 feet (220 by 230 meters). It is one of the largest ancient structures in Earth's **Western Hemisphere**.

Archaeologists aren't sure what the pyramid was used for. A wooden temple may have stood on the top as a **roof comb**. The priests of Teotihuacán might have used it to worship the Great Goddess of Teotihuacán. Painted murals found in the city show that she took the form of a spider.

Great Goddess

*Some people think the Pyramid of the Sun originally had 260 steps. This number is significant to other ancient **Indigenous** peoples. For example, the Mayan calendar featured a 260-day cycle.*

THE PYRAMID OF THE MOON

The Pyramid of the Moon is the second-tallest structure in Teotihuacán. Its main stairway faces the Avenue of the Dead. It is 140 feet (43 meters) high. Its base is 426 feet by 511 feet (130 by 156 meters). It was built between 100 and 400 CE.

Skeletons have been uncovered around and below this pyramid. They include the remains of humans, jaguars, wolves, and eagles. The bodies appear to have been **sacrificed** during religious rituals.

HOW CAN THEY TELL?

There is evidence at these archaeological sites that early civilizations in **Mesoamerica** practiced human sacrifice. For example, tests on the soil and bones from an Aztec ball game court showed human blood and male neck bones. The bones showed evidence of having been cut through by something sharp. This means the players likely had their heads chopped off.

THE TEMPLE OF THE FEATHERED SERPENT

The Temple of the Feathered Serpent is decorated with stone heads of the snake-bird god. Evidence shows the walls were once painted red. Hundreds of human skeletons have been found in pits around the temple. Some of them were dressed as warriors. In 2003, a large sinkhole opened near the temple. Archaeologists explored the opening. They found a tunnel leading beneath the pyramid. Before digging, archaeologists spent nearly a year creating a digital map of the underground tunnels and chambers using **LiDAR** scanners.

LiDAR scanners use a laser beam to measure the distance between it and solid objects underground, such as a wall or floor.

Crews of archaeologists helped excavate the tunnel. Robots assisted them digging out 1,000 tons (907 metric tons) of soil. Over more than 10 years of work, they discovered at least 100,000 **artifacts** dating back to Aztec times. They found jaguar bones, crocodile teeth, and human skin. They found finely carved statues and ornate pieces of pottery. There were precious jewels and rare shells. A small model of the nearby mountain range was discovered along with pools of poisonous mercury. There were even wooden objects that had survived the centuries.

Tunnel of the Stars

One tunnel had a ceiling that glittered like the night sky. Scientists found it contained metals called pyrite and magnetite which reflect light and can look like twinkling stars. Not found in this region, the Aztecs brought these metals from somewhere else and used them to paint the tunnel ceiling.

RULE OF THE AZTECS

By the time the Aztecs discovered Teotihuacán, they had already become an impressive society. Aztec culture centered around their capital city Tenochtitlán, which means "place of the prickly pear cactus." They ruled central and southern Mexico from 1325 to about 1500 CE. The Aztecs also built temples in the shape of pyramids in Tenochtitlán. The final Aztec emperor, Moctezuma II, had a great palace there, with two zoos.

This sketch shows the ancient city of Tenochtitlán as it was before the Spanish arrived. Built on a small island, legend says an Aztec god told them to build their city where they saw an eagle on a cactus eating a snake.

The Aztecs believed Teotihuacán was a holy place. Its name means "birthplace of the gods." The ruins became an important religious center for the Aztecs who made **pilgrimages** to the ruins to honor their gods. Although the Aztecs claimed to be descended from the builders of Teotihuacán, evidence suggests that the builders were a culture unique from the Aztecs and ancient Maya.

TEOTIHUACÁN LOST AGAIN

When the Spanish arrived there in 1519, they battled with the Aztecs for years. After Tenochtitlán fell to them, the Spanish built their own city atop its ruins. Mexico became a colony of Spain until the Mexican people won their battle for independence in 1821. During that period, Teotihuacán was largely ignored by the Spanish rulers and once again the city was forgotten. It was not until the 20th century that serious archaeological excavations began, revealing the ancient city's magnitude.

At first, Aztec emperor Moctezuma welcomed Spanish ***conquistador*** *Hernán Cortés and his men to Tenochtitlán. Moctezuma made the fatal mistake of thinking that Cortés was the god Quetzalcoatl.*

A WALK THROUGH HISTORY

Today, tourists can visit Teotihuacán and see its magnificent pyramids. People are no longer allowed to climb the ancient structures. But they can stroll along the Avenue of the Dead and imagine what life was like in the bustling city over a thousand years ago.

For now, excavations at Teotihuacán are complete. Researchers are busy studying the enormous amount of evidence uncovered at the site. Bones are being analyzed for information about the people who once lived there. Plans are being made to someday unearth more of the city's treasures. Researchers continue to discover clues that help tell the story of the mysterious pyramids the Aztecs found so long ago.

OLD AND NEW

Teotihuacán is just 30 miles (50 kilometers) away from modern-day Mexico City. The site is Mexico's most popular tourist attraction. Nearly four and a half million visitors come each year.

GLOSSARY

archaeologists (ahr-kee-AH-luh-juhsts) Scientists who study the distant past by digging up things that people made, used, and left behind

artifacts (AHR-tuh-fakts) Objects made and used by humans in the past, including tools and weapons

civilizations (siv-uh-li-ZAY-shuhnz) Groups of people with their own language and way of life

conquistador (kahn-KEE-stuh-dor) A person from Spain who sought to conquer the New World, find treasure there, and convert its people to Christianity; Spanish for conqueror

excavations (EK-skuh-vay-shuhnz) Projects that involve digging in the soil to uncover objects

Indigenous (in-DIJ-uh-nuhs) Referring to the original inhabitants of a particular place

LiDAR (LYE-dar) Short for Light Detection and Ranging

Mesoamerica (mez-oh-uh-MAIR-ih-kuh) An historic area that was home to civilizations before the arrival of Christopher Columbus, which included modern-day Nicaragua, northern Costa Rica, Honduras, El Salvador, Guatemala, Belize, and central to southern Mexico

metropolis (muh-TRAH-puh-luhs) A very large city, often the most important city in a region

pilgrimage (PIL-gruh-mij) A long journey to a holy or sacred place

plateau (pla-TOH) Flat ground that is higher than the surrounding area

priests (preests) Religious people who can perform ceremonies and rituals

roof comb (roof kohm) A wall rising from the center line of a roof to give an appearance of greater height

sacrificed (SAK-ruh-ficed) Killed or gave up something valuable, as a trade for something you want; offered to a god

underworld (UN-duhr-wurld) The mythical world of the dead believed to be underground

Western Hemisphere (WEST-ern HEM-ih-sfeer) The part of Earth consisting of North and South America and the waters around them.

INDEX

archaeologists 8, 16, 21, 23

Avenue of the Dead 10, 18, 28

Aztecs 8, 10, 23, 24, 25, 26, 28

civilizations 5, 8, 12

excavations 14, 26, 28

gods 8, 21, 25, 26

metropolis 8, 12

Moctezuma II 24, 26

Pyramid of the Moon 5, 10, 14, 18

Pyramid of the Sun 5, 11, 14, 16

sacrifices 18, 19

San Juan River 10

skeletons 18, 21

Spanish 24, 26

Temple of the Feathered Serpent 5, 11, 14

Tenochtitlán 24, 26

tourists 28, 29

tunnels 21

underworld 14

volcanoes 6

QUESTIONS AFTER READING

1. The tallest pyramid at Teotihuacán is _____.
   a. The Pyramid of the Moon
   b. The Pyramid of the Sun
   c. The Temple of the Feathered Serpent

2. Teotihuacán was named by ______
   a. archaeologists
   b. an unknown ancient civilization
   c. the Aztecs

3. Teotihuacán was once one of the ______ cities in the world.
   a. most peaceful
   b. smallest
   c. largest

4. ____ have not been found at Teotihuacán.
   a. Royal tombs
   b. Skeletons
   c. Murals

5. Stone heads of the snake-bird god decorate ______.
   a. The Pyramid of the Moon
   b. The Pyramid of the Sun
   c. The Temple of the Feathered Serpent

Answers: 1. b, 2. c, 3. c, 4. a, 5. c

ABOUT THE AUTHOR

Murray "Oak" Tapeta was born in a toilet-less cabin in Montana. Growing up in the great outdoors, he learned to love trees. He got the nickname "Oak" after climbing to the top of an oak tree when he was only three years old. Oak loves to read and write. He has written a number of books about fascinating, terrible, and gruesome events from the distant past. He prefers spending time in the wilderness with his dog, Birchy.

Author: Murray "Oak" Tapeta

Editor: Kathy Middleton

Proofreader: Crystal Sikkens

Design: Samara Parent and Kathy Walsh

Production coordinator: Candice Campbell

IMAGE CREDITS

Alamy: ©Zuma Press, Inc: p 22-23; ©Everett Collection Inc: p 26-27

Shutterstock: ©Mohammed_Al_Ali, p 7 (second from top); ©Natalia Golovina: p 13; ©Thomas Aleto from Riverside, P: p 17 (top); ©Santiago Castillo Chomel: p 19 (bottom right); © quiggyt4: p 20-21; ©Stan Design BIM: p 21 (bottom right); ©Anamaria Mejia: p 28-29; ©SkyCamAerials: p 29 (top right)

Wikimedia Commons: ©Gary Todd from Xinzheng, China: p 24-25

All other images from Shutterstock

Crabtree Publishing

crabtreebooks.com **800-387-7650**

In Canada: We acknowledge the financial support of the Government of Canada through the Canada Book Fund for our publishing activities.

Hardcover 978-1-0398-7283-7
Paperback 978-1-0398-7341-4
Ebook (pdf) 978-1-0398-7396-4
Epub 978-1-0398-7445-9

Published in Canada
Crabtree Publishing
616 Welland Avenue
St. Catharines, Ontario
L2M 5V6

Published in the United States
Crabtree Publishing
347 Fifth Avenue
Suite 1402-145
New York, New York, 10016

Library and Archives Canada Cataloguing in Publication
Available at Library and Archives Canada

Library of Congress Cataloging-in-Publication Data
Available at the Library of Congress

Printed in the U.S.A./CP052026